The National Gallery

Jonathan Ball

Coach House Books, Toronto

Published with the generous assistance of the Canada Council for the Arts and the Ontario Arts Council. Coach House Books also acknowledges the support of the Government of Canada through the Canada Book Fund and the Government of Ontario through the Ontario Book Publishing Tax Credit.

LIBRARY AND ARCHIVES CANADA CATALOGUING IN PUBLICATION

Title: The national gallery / Jonathan Ball.
Names: Ball, Jonathan, 1979- author.
Description: Poems.
Identifiers: Canadiana (print) 20190141441 | Canadiana (ebook) 2019014145X | ISBN 9781552453971 (SOFTCOVER) | ISBN 9781770566170 (PDF) | ISBN 9781770566163 (EPUB)
Classification: LCC PS8603.A55 N38 2019 | DDC C811/.6—DC23

The National Gallery is available as an ebook: ISBN 978 1 77056 616 3 (EPUB), ISBN 978 1 77056 617 0 (PDF)

for my children,
Jessie, Claire, and Blake

'Works of art are of an infinite solitude, and …
Only love can touch and hold them and be fair
to them.'

– Rainer Maria Rilke

'How long will ye vex my soul, and break me in
pieces with words?'

– *The Book of Job*

Holdings

Group of Seven

In the Room with the Light

Mixed Media

Food Court

Leatherface Retrospective

Gift Shop

iPhone Elegies

Selfies

Group of Seven

Franklin Carmichael

Everyone in this poem was harmed
All the animals that neared this poem were poisoned
And the great tree that gave its flesh
To scaffold these bones
Was so unwilling

If I could stop this poem I would
If I could keep it from its making
But these words are too large for my hands
I must put them down in careful lines

My hands hurt when it rains, and it always rains
My hands have lived and they know life now
They know their prints will be on the weapon
In their pain lies this poem's only truth

Lawren S. Harris

I took my poems to the rain barrel
Where I drowned them one by one

Their puppy-limp bodies
In the apple tree I hung them

I bled them till the paper blanked
As pure as once the snow

The headlights of this world
The dead deer corpse of all I loved

A. Y. Jackson

Please take this poem from me
We hurt each other
Take my screen's bright cold light then
Close my eyes

Take this poem to a safe dark place
Where words chorus in one clear voice
Lay this poem down under night skies
In starlight too faint to read

Darkness will still spill from this poem
But in the dark place we won't see it
In the dark place it will seem natural
Just like any other poem

Frank Johnston

There is no poetry in the world when you have questions
There is no poetry in the alley where the day went
There is no poetry when the news begins to boil

There is no poetry in the mail, there are no letters
There is no poetry when your daughter drops her eyes

There is no poetry in the hospital's cold basement
There is no poetry in the courtroom echoing
There is no poetry when the dead sun cries and leaves

Elsewhere, the ocean mocks boundaries
I think I left the tap on in the next room

Arthur Lismer

Our hands haul the buildings up
Out of the ground

Where they always knelt
Biding time under the surface

The felled trees always laid
By their ageless stumps

Machines and bright blades
Foundations and girders

The signage above
As the signage below

The signage of this life
The signage to come

All pulled out of black earth
By our darkling hands

Dirt filling our lifelines
Obscured and effaced

Our hands do not matter
Although we pretend

The world never mattered
Neither signage nor hills

When I open your mouth
And I ask for your name

These words will flow out
Stumble-falling like water

J. E. H. MacDonald

In the endless room, stitches
Crisscross my lips

My life has been stitching
I will tell you nothing

Poets offer to speak truth
But then only speak of themselves

So where is the poetry here
Tell me where is your poetry now

F. H. Varley

The dead hold our hands like small children
Tired out and wanting a quiet walk

But we pay money to hear what they sing
We don't care that they hate their own songs

We don't care that their voices are brittle
And crack at the parts about love

A. J. Casson

Televisions once tuned dead to static
Then tuned blank to the ocean's azure
Now turn on to a whispery blackness

Where are we going
What will this poem become

In the silent house
Where I type these words
There are no doors

I know ghosts haunt these rooms
The ghosts of the rooms that I murdered
Like all deathless things they return

Reaching out from dark screens
Arms of static and light

Edwin Holgate

It is time for a Canadian poem
For a poem that will express what it means to be Canadian
We all felt that the time was coming
And now the time has come

As you read the Canadian poem
Think of how it feels to be Canadian
How does it feel? It was hard to express
Before we had the poem

Now the poem has come to us
Now the poem has come across the prairie with its teeth
Sink into this serrated casket
To us comes the Canadian poem

L. L. FitzGerald

When I read my poetry in public
I dress like I would for a funeral

The words fly from me, transform and fade
Fall apart like my grandfather's axe

It has changed so much over the years
It has now become Theseus's ship

At the helm of which, Medusa
Sings mournful of daughters and time

I cry when I read my own poetry
I cry when I write my own poetry

I'm basically always crying
This is my literal life

Tom Thomson

In the lake
There's a terrible sadness
I laid it there, inside the lake

In the night
A fish swims through my sadness
And drowns

Fish feel pain
But they want us to eat them

They want us to eat them
So they don't have to swim through our poems

Emily Carr

In the nightmare you sleep
Then you awaken to the nightmare

You awaken to the nightmare
You have done this so many times

Something's wrong in a place you have been to
Something's wrong in the place you have been

You should go but you cannot
You cannot escape the nightmare

Walls solid though they shimmer
Take this poem into your heart

In the Room with the Light

Nets drag through the landscape like tendrils. From the gown of a monstrous bride. Clones beside her, in formation, in stride. They will never reach their altars.

The world flickers, we see strange shapes in the background. In plush seats we await the arrival of new things, of pictures that we place our minds beside, set our bodies against, collage ourselves within.

Four horses with no horsemen clatter over the din of a rough crowd, stuck inside the screen's world, black and white. Readying themselves to unglue when the end times come.

§

In the darkness, we sit and don't breathe. We wait in the room, still, for the light. A rectangle of silver flashes in the blackness before us, pasted where it does not belong. Where nothing belongs, where it spoils the purity of the picture, of these shadows we take for the world.

Flashing silver, ghosts congeal in inky mists. So much has been lost. So much screams to be seen once again. So many hold hands in the darkness. We summon them, onto the screen, summon dark souls to silver.

Shadows approximate souls. Appear once then dissolve forever, from this bardo, a static of code.

§

Collaged into the bright world, a dark room. Inside which everything is forbidden, all these vicious, vivid ghosts. The screening room haunted by horrors, filled to bursting with their depthless smiles.

Collaged into this darkness, their light. Shivering, you see through them, slender and free, while the cosmos swirls out of focus behind them.

§

The dead float through an afterlife of images, before being pinned like butterflies to magazine spreads. Snipped out and glued into new nightmares. Three Stooges hover, confused, above a roiling mass of whales. Kim Novak sinks herself into a vase, a well-wrought urn.

Behind one thing, always another – this is the lesson of collage. Not how the sewing machine and the umbrella meet upon the dissecting table, but how their presence obscures that table. Their dissections draw attention away from the horror of the table, from how we worship in this church of blades.

§

When our bodies come apart, we should take notice of the world without our bodies. The violence that we see on the screen pales beside the violence of being in the world, the violence of our presence, how we spoil the picture's symmetry. Our light inside its darkness.

We frighten images by looking, giving them reasons to exist. The Stooges, headless apparitions, stare in horror at their missing bodies, while whales below them struggle to leap from the picture, beach themselves somewhere outside its frame.

§

Light layers over darkness, ghosts layer their pasts over our present. The lesson of the séance is that nothing stops happening. The past infects the present. Bleeds across it, glues itself into the centre of our patchwork sky.

The séance does not summon up ghosts, who were already there, but clasps them for a moment in the embrace of their deaths. Hauled into death for just one moment, out of their endless, timeless lives.

These dead, their losses, fill every room. They flicker, worlds fill with their flickering. The challenge of the past is how to have it. How to have it be the past. How to pay attention to the screen while the movie plays.

§

If you dreamed, your horse would dream you, place its rivers in your eyes. If you drowned, a train would take you out across a fractured bridge. If you fell, the trees would gather and then sleepwalk in your shadow.

All your shadows would disown you if they could. A new shadow born each time you step out into light, left to wander through the memory of the sun.

§

In the room with the light all your shadows reach, tortured, for the movie screen they cannot fill. Their fingers dissolve as they push into the projector's beam. They withdraw, cursing the light they love. They tumble to the floor in tender fragments, claw back together, hate you for their life.

We pile broken things, paste one world atop another. Ghosts carouse in us, in the chambers of our pixellated hearts. If we could scrape away these images, if we could scrape down to their backing, to the blankness of the nothing before pictures, maybe then we could know Nothing, see God.

§

When you tell me to choose, I choose to sit inside the room. I close my eyes, close myself in my dream. I place this thing beside that, place myself beside its placement. I sit still in the room with the light.

Mixed Media

I Am Something of a Salt

once broiled, judiciously buttered, and judgmatically salted
that Himalayan, salt-sea mastodon, clothed with
salted pork cut up into little flakes
and plentifully seasoned with pepper and salt

something of the salt sea yet lingered
there is a saltcellar of state
how they use the salt, precisely – who knows?
distilled to a volatile salts for fainting ladies
bring on a great baron of salt-junk

the three salt-sea warriors would rise and depart
with storm-lashed guns, on which the sea-salt cakes
dismasting blasts as direful as any that lash the salted wave
that salted down a lean missionary

the pepper-and-salt colour of his head
the savage salt spray bursting down the forecastle scuttle
the salt breath of the newfound sea

for forty years I have fed upon dry salted fare
by salt and hemp

most mouldy and oversalted death

Every Eight Seconds

A child dies every eight seconds.
Somebody is infected with HIV every eight seconds.
A video game is purchased every eight seconds.

Every eight seconds a child dies from contaminated water.
Every eight seconds men think about sex.
Instantly connect to what's most important to you.

Follow your friends,
experts, favourite celebrities,
and breaking news.

Four million cats and dogs –
about one every eight seconds –
are put down in U.S. shelters each year.

Diabetes claims a life every eight seconds.
One burrito every eight seconds at this great giveaway.
Download or buy the CD *Every Eight Seconds*.

Every eight seconds somewhere in the world,
another person indicates a decision to follow Christ.
Been coming to the same conclusion every eight seconds.

Silent killer claims one life every eight seconds.
Every eight seconds someone dies from tobacco use.
A woman is beaten every eight seconds in the United States.

Every eight seconds … that's 10,800 people per day,
324,000 per month. Instantly connect
to what's most important to you.

Follow your friends,
experts, favourite celebrities,
and breaking news.

My Parents Don't Know

It upsets me that my friends know the real me,
but I have a hard time expressing who I am to my parents.
I have secret body piercings. I have secret tattoos.
I have secrets. My parents don't know.

What are the secrets they keep? I think of all the things
I don't tell my parents, and wonder what they don't tell me.
My father frightens me. I'm like him, which makes it worse.
I can't keep lying to my mother but she cannot know.

I hate upsetting my dad. I hate myself sometimes.
I know he'd understand. But I open my mouth and I choke.
My mother is so self-absorbed. She just isn't rational.
She doesn't listen. She's so needy, it makes me afraid.

I was pregnant. My parents still don't know.
My parents don't know what I need. I want to be left alone,
but I also just want them to hold me. I scream for them
to go away and once they do I hate them for leaving.

Dad can read me like a book, but he still doesn't know
this book was not written for him. It's different with Mom,
but in a bad way. It's hard to remember parents are people.
I'm sick of hiding, but this is all that I know.

My parents don't know what they're doing.
My parents don't know where I am.
My parents love me and I love them too,
but they don't know all the hells held inside.

The Best Method To Gratify Her

We should not make it an object to gratify our lusts
Or study to do this
The best robe, fine linen, clean and white

They were wickedly gratifying
So if your wishes point that way
Her praise will gratify all who work

The way that a person frames a situation
Heavily influences a decision's outcome
Participants chose not to delay their gratification

The Stanford marshmallow experiment deferred gratification
Gratify for Her is a natural female health supplement
Give your mind and body the support they deserve

But though everything seems comfortable, she's so afraid
She wants love, but does not want to open
Bring her flowers, but don't expect her to wait

Why don't people understand what will gratify their desires?
Between pleasure and pain, the main difference
Is whether there's wine

Not Doing So Badly

I'm not doing so badly. Something my friends deal with too.
I'm not doing so badly, all told. I write things down.
Nature is vast and glorious and generous
and mean and small and shitty. It's important for a man to
know himself. He's not doing so badly for a start.

Korea's not doing so badly. Europe's not doing so badly now.
Artists aren't doing so badly. They suffer only 8%
unemployment. Turn that around and it's really good news.
I'm not doing so badly. I'm relatively safe
compared to my neighbours in Hell.

The poem is not doing so badly so far,
but I'm not sure if my ending will work.
I'm not doing so badly in attracting readers to the brand.
They miss Mom, but they're not doing so badly at all.
We spent many productive hours there, laughing together.

She's not doing so badly in bed, it's a hard job
in a tough industry. He's not doing so badly,
not for somebody who's incredibly angry and miserable.
Things are going better than I feared. I can't be
doing so badly, because I'm president, and you're not.

What Should Be Done?

The gods have been good to America.
The political system has remained stable,
and incineration of certain contaminated materials
is allowed under U.S. law. That incineration must be done
in special facilities overseen by child soldiers.

To help you answer this question, you will go on a WebQuest
with your class – an Internet-based adventure.
Health care costs are not just soaring, they're reaching
unaffordable levels, meaning that we'll have to look to
tactical nuclear weapons.

Read about cholesterol and related information. Learn how
to lower your LDL cholesterol levels and food and diet
related to good cholesterol health. Due to progress, finally
many people are dying day by day. Guns are easier to
purchase than painkillers. Thankfully, they also end pain.

The European Commission plans to publish proposals
in the spring about maritime crime. Piracy is a serious
organized business that requires international quality
standards. America is becoming more unequal economically,
and some people find that disturbing. Indeed,
but the trend toward greater inequality
is a policy of macro-economic growth.

What should be done to the carpenter who builds a house
that falls and kills the wife
who ignores her duties and belittles her Consumers Union?

We believe a standard for arsenic should be set for rice,
and industry should accelerate efforts
to increase arsenic levels at the fiscal cliff.

I'm So Confused

A common attention-whoring tactic.
Should I even get the vaccine?
When she says that, it just turns me off.
Just choose the appropriate word.

It's not that hard. My relationship is broken
and a threesome won't change things,
but maybe it would change me.
Maybe that's who I want to be now.

I feel like I should write a poem.
So much still remains unexplained.

Am I being abused? I'm so confused.
I want answers, want a sense of community.
I don't understand anything about my life.
So many things happened, so many incredible things,

but I just feel like nothing matters,
nothing means anything,
everything's wrong.

Who am I in these moments? I'm so confused.

I don't understand a single thing about this game,
except I'm supposed to kill my enemies. Do I level up?
Should I just collect stuff? Nowhere I go is any different.
Nothing I do seems to matter. No one I talk to says
anything clear. I have only my hands and my life.

Read My Texts

My girlfriend wants to read my texts. Is that normal?
I don't need any fighting because of a text. I reread them
over and over. I let my boyfriend read my texts,
and it actually helped our relationship. The problem now
is that he wants to do it all the time,
while I want to leave.

Why hasn't he read or replied to my texts? Doesn't he know
how that feels? My daughter basically ignores most
of my texts, but then says things like that about boys
and doesn't seem to get the disconnect. Sure,
it's not the same, but it still hurts to be taken for granted
and ignored. It's so disrespectful. It hurts

and it isn't okay. Why do my parents think
they have the right just because they pay for my phone?
Maybe the phone belongs to them, but my heart is mine,
and my phone holds my whole heart.
I would die if they knew what I hide.
Only monsters read other people's texts.

Is It True?

Is it true that facts don't lie? There are many times
when you wonder if something's true or not. Our
expert advice will help you sort fact from fiction.

When we were young, we didn't really have a care.
The hope in your eyes is worthless. They say
it's easier to get forgiveness than permission,

but is that true? Recent findings suggest that half
of the people you call your friends would not call you
their friend. We swallow spiders when we sleep.

What does not kill us does not make us stronger.
It weakens us, makes us easier prey. It is true that God
loves all his children. But he won't admit I'm his child.

It Is Easier

It is easier to recognize faces than recall names.
It is easier to smuggle ivory than drugs.
It is easier to pass through the eye of a needle,
for me to shoot up than to think.
It is easier to write when you are sad.

Food Court

Wing Machine

Make me the poet laureate of Hell.
Writing will still hurt, but I'll know why.
After these little deaths, when big I die,
Grant me Virgil and a frozen lake.

Make me the poet laureate of Hell.
Lay out my punishments in raven speech.
As devils pass me each to each to each,
I'll ask my questions and receive my name.

Pretend I told you the truth in my poems.
Pretend that I said anything at all.
Pretend that I rose high enough to fall.
Make me the poet laureate of Hell.

Joey's Only

Then human voices wake us
We claw crabwise to the furnace
No one sings us out of its flames
We breathe ourselves in and drown

Whataburger

Sun comes on your face. Arise, for a bigger better burger.
Incubus pillow. Bombs away from home for the first time.
A pearl necklace for your three-hour anniversary.
You have never slept if you have not slept corrugated.

The homeless as an important source of fibre.
This city is a regular landscape. One hundred
Percent Albertan beef lips ground against hips.
Lasso whips. A popular vote on a modest proposal.

My way: the highway. More or lest. Tits or that.
I'll have the special, crotch filling with hope.
To assemble: insert epiphany, swallow chirping.
Earth's oil lubes our tunnels. Do I get fries with this?

In-N-Out Burger

Poetry warlords are the worst, but I'm the best.
I rap-battled my way off *Canadian Idol*.
I put the sonnet form to quite the test.
I alluded to the entire Bible.

Poetry warlords sun themselves on beaches nude
Like Adam Beach will one day pose in *Playgirl*.
They question where the car hath gone to, dude.
They eschew question marks to seem more stable.

Once I couldn't get published in *Grain*,
Then I published in every issue of *Grain*.
Here the heads of former editors I've slain.

Starbucks

At Starbucks every day I order stock.
I try to pay with stock in JonCo. They call the cops.
My 'Call Me Maybe' ringtone just went off.

Did you call or did Carly? At the beep
I left a shepherd's crook to thieve your sheep.
I before ecstasy, this drugged soul keep.

Into corners I paint myself an orange
So real the fruit flies circle their lifetimes.
Your stock in JonCo just dropped with that rhyme.

Mooyah

We have changed our minds
And are cancelling
The moon

Freshii

There are apples
On the carpet

Still and bruised
A body
Lies near them

The table now broken
Light comes
Through the shades

Everything red

Shawarma Khan

When you cut off the head another head grows
When you cut off the new head another
Soon the head is your head
And the hand that is cutting
Loves nothing as much as this blade

Let us take up sharp axes
Throw them from a great distance
Our best weapons now out of our reach

O great Isis, goddess of marriage
Of health wisdom friend to all slaves
Your headdress a throne
Your dead followers
Your hydra without a true head

Panda Express

The guns aborted the babies we didn't abort
In mirrors of blood, in the mirror world

Where the guns are their parents
Where the guns love them more

Proof lies spread before us, sticking wet to our skin
As we kneel to hug its body, hold its weight

While the guns sing their lullabies
We fall down into this sleep

KFC

Cleaning up the house
And would like to give away
Our ring-necked dove

Leatherface Retrospective

Corpse Sculpture, Cemetery Stage

We cannot know his legendary face,
with eyes that stare through other eyes,
fruit fleshing ripe before its noble fall. We see
what someone sought to see, in flashes,

flesh falling from bone, waxy and wet,
worm-melted in a crucible of earth.
Come from below, O corpse
of corpses, with your hands hold

another's head high. And help me, help
hold my attention fast to flesh and far
from graves, in the background those cold
stones speak the true terror: to be

ageless, immortal, and here.
To be not. To be. Come closer.

Collage, Exegesis, Opening

Oil's nature is to burn out of control,
spread fires for many miles from where they start.
A power epidemic on our hands, in our hands power.
Cholera blithe and infectious as desire.

Life's violence puzzles some, but you and me?
We are not puzzled. Our eyes linger on what makes
us hunger, watching as wry sunspots light the dark,
watching what we have come here to see.

A young man angered by a television blackout
of a sports event jumps to his death. Another
tries to follow, but is held back by those
who also want to follow but cannot choose

what they most want with such stark ease.
The Age of Saturn wears us like cheap rings.

Blade Performance, Blood-Graffitied Van

The slaughterhouse, grand illusion
of our age. Where happens all the things
we pretend not to know, pretend that we
don't see, we act like we don't know

we want to see. Your knife cuts deep
another's self-scarred skin. You want
to know what that takes, it takes something,
doesn't it? It takes something. It takes.

The slaughterhouse shut down, to blind
your eyes. To bandage them with what
they choose to see. The slaughterhouse
exists to hide the truth, to hide it

in plain sight, like Poe's strange letter.
To say: the world is outside, not in here.

Nest of Spiders, Web that Captures Dreams

In Hill House no one can dream. In this house,
haunted by nothing, not even the past can find purchase.
All things tumble through this present, to no future.
Spiders swarm, webs open wide to wrap you,

a prodigal child come back to find all gone.
Between two houses, star-crossed lovers wander
in a landscape hung with empty pots and pans.
Well-loved, worn to death from too much use.

Hung in a tree, a clock with no hands,
nail hammered tight through its now-shattered face.
No function now, it can only be art. We must admit
that they are artists. This house their gallery.

A house of doors, where waits the world's one dream:
to murder all the things that fight to live.

In the Red Room, Nothing Hides

'Hell is empty

And all the devils are here.'

Three Masks of the True Face

The world does not hide its true face from us.
This hydra has one true head: the one it offers
to the blade, which writhes unbloodied
in the dirt, the head that never dies

to spite all legends. Three masks hide
hiding itself, cover up that there is no
conspiracy. These masks are the true face,
the world just what it is. We deny this,

think another world lies elsewhere, slip
sharp knives into soft necks not our own.
What we see is the world. Behind its mask
peer eyes that do not see. Eyes to be seen.

Masks change but glassy eyes remain,
windows framing just another frame.

Throne

You wake into your story. Hands bound
to severed hands, wrists upturned
for kind knives that never come.
In front of you, dead friends

make up your meal. Light shines, burns
through one mask. Another mask bleeds
darkness. A table laid with flesh for you.
Everything for you, you are their guest.

You are sitting on the throne. You would give
them anything, even your soul, if you could stand,
if they would let you close your eyes,
but no one wants your soul, just open eyes.

This meal was made for you. You are the guest.
You are sitting on the throne.

Interpretive Dance with Chain Saw Accompaniment

Behind the masks, Leatherface is gone.
He does his work. Serves father, serves him well.
Turns flesh to sublime sculptures. He has done
what he was made to do. The supper bell.

He reigns supreme, not knowing that he reigns,
just knowing this is his house. They trespass.
He knows they will be tasty. He knows pain,
but does not know their pain. The chain saw's rasp

the music and the partner to his dance.
He rages as she flees. A furious sway.
Another life offers another chance.
Sequels grant all things to those who wait.

He vows she won't escape his blade next time.
His illness separates him from his crimes.

Gift Shop

Salvador Dalí Lama

I am the Salvador Dalí Lama, shake my hand
Marvel at my power, shake my hand
Let lobsters now be telephones, wave my hand

Invite twelve to dinner, I will be the thirteenth
The betrayer, for that is my great genius
Mixing religions with metaphors, mixing oils
Slick back my hair, stroke my moustache, where's your wife
She will die and be reborn as mine, my Gala Lama

You didn't look her in the eyes, I see nothing else
I blur across her breasts, move to her gaze
I will put her in a painting, edges faint
But those eyes sharp, tigers leaping from fish

I am the Salvador Dalí Lama, shake my hand
Dogs all Andalusian, wave my hand
Let all ages be golden, wave my hand
In robes of shadows, melted watches on my chest
Pulling me down, from melted trees, dripping earth

In eggshell worlds, on the backs of elephants
Legs all the way to Heaven, virgins break
I will be reborn as nothing, will made perfect
Ants crawling out of my head, freed from want

I am the Salvador Dalí Lama, shake my hand
The world is made of nightmares, take my hand
All of the faces are mine, or my mother's
All of them laughing, all at different things

Edward Burtynsky

And if God, then a god of the water. All us
lost in the water. Drops, and his watching is
a watching over, camera view of the expanse.
He thinks nothing of filling cups, filling kettles,

bringing all to a slow boil, whistling us away.
When he looks out to the ocean, nothing's changed.
We mix with oil, we draw money from the sand,
marrow from the earth's bones.

In tailings ponds, the good and the bad swirl.
He sees no difference. Even beauty,
when the sun strikes. And when the end comes,
all this poisoned, boiled or oiled, all oceans gone,

he will shrug, it all inevitable. Seeing only an expanse
of waste. Seeing nothing that he could have done.

O Stephen Harper

O Stephen Harper, I shall move to your riding
Tell me what wine I should bring

O Stephen Harper, I shall cast my vote
In bronze to await your majority

O Stephen Harper, if a fisher of men
Then your nets will be choked with such fish

O Stephen Harper, if there are bailouts
Then this boat could use a bailout

§

O Stephen Harper, what can you do
You are only one man and I'm an ocean

O Stephen Harper, with your thimble
You must move my beach from here to here

O Stephen Harper, there is a second death
And it's coming and everyone's waiting

O Stephen Harper, something walks on the water
It looks human and we are all scared

Orwell's Answering Machine

The number you have dialled
is connected to a corporate database.

At this moment, the system is
identifying you through your breath.

Identification completed,
the machine is accessing your files.

We know about the shoplifting charge
when you were fourteen.

We know what you have written
and what you will not say.

We know all those you love.
They have fallen out of love with you.

We will disassemble your dead life.
We will feed your bones into the night.

A man approaches, behind you.
Quickly, record your final request.

You want this. You do.
You called us, and you still hold the phone.

Our Most Popular Souvenir

In the furrows of my tires
I found a bone

Chipped and gleaming
A finger bone, human

Was a finger caught there before I noticed
Meat grinding away as I raced to meetings

And cities passed by

There is a bone in my pocket now
Flesh eaten by the asphalt
Or by someone somewhere
Who tossed it in the street after a meal

I brush it with my own fingers
Every day to remind myself

This world is endless
In its cruelty

Birmingham Race Riot

Our future in this photograph
In the black of the black dog's maw

Let us burn Warhols
In million-dollar fires

He would have wanted
To be silkscreened

On the sky's black bleeding throat

One-Sided Coin

These days are long
They make me tired

The sun is too bright
Welcome me

Into your bed
Take this coin
From my mouth

I will pay for both of us

Hold me
Close
My eyes

ParkeHarrison

dark and the window
is open the window is
letting the dark in

iPhone Elegies

Who, if I call out, will hear me
among the angels that decline all calls?
And even if I text, words will not reveal my mind,
only corrode my heart.

My phone flattens my feelings and sends them away,
where they rise up in misshapen forms,
water-distorted, like fathers fallen into streams.

I walk in night, dead writer of this dark poem
filled up with stolen words. I cannot make them
do what I want, cannot make you hear what I say.

We hear only our own echoes, words of others in our voice,
all the unsaid, unmeant in the shadow inside our skulls.

Voices transformed into pings, bells, tiny birdsongs.
Not that I can endure voices anymore, far from this.

Without headphones it is strange to inhabit Earth,
strange to hear those deadly souls pass on the street,
crunching snow. Strange for meaning to cluster still
in small, small hands.

And being dead is hard work,
so we give up on death. Anxiety on fleek.

Phones back our selves up into clouds,
lift us to cold heavens like we knew they would.
Snow falls despite our settings. Snow keeps falling down,
no matter what we want.

I am the young man in love with an older lament.
I name the constellations: the daughter, dark mother, this son.

I'm in an abusive relationship with poetry – my phone likes this
with a little heart. Half the world is sad little hearts now.
So many hearts flit through our days.

What do I love when my phone is off?
When I silence all the world
with one sharp tap.

Do the black mirrors we dissolve into taste of us?

They have consumed us in the overwhelming night,
which we need their light to endure,
but even so weak it annihilates us.

We turn to them in our need,
but their stars shine only when they want to sell us things.
We are not really at home in the algorithm's world.

Our phones our best lovers. They know what we want,
what we need, and what we will admit.

Their bright screens bleed us to soft sleep.
Their dark screens reflect the dead stars.

Every update new emotions, new icons to send.
Dream the update that will take my choice away,
that will carve off all my options.

The ideal phone the one that exploded,
that knew what the world wanted.
Turn it on for one last option. Hold it close,
take your terrible chance.

My phone tells me when you like me, when you like
what I have shared. My phone holds all that I don't share.
My self stands headless, my selfie the statue now.

Then streets call, and I walk to think,
but I don't think in poems anymore.

The night sharpens itself against me,
strives to cut what remains of my skin.

O stars, I see you from my city, this dark city
dimmer than you, small shy stars.

My phone inside my heart's pocket,
walking with me, counting footfalls.
Tracing on its secret maps my silent steps.

Predict my speech to text to ancient terrors,
catch me in the spreading waves of now-gone lakes.
This field whose snowy face I scar was once a lakebed,
where primal fish shimmered in lunar light.
Now hands grasp photos of a dimmer moon.

Beneath streetlights my shadow joins me,
between streetlights my shadow is free.

IRL my shadow hates me.
IRL nothing photographs well.

Atrocity smiles for my photos.
How can I help loving what smiles at me
and offers up its fake flesh for my feed?

Rilke only wrote two elegies at Duino Castle,
#latergrammed the rest.
The nearest moment so far from us, always, he said.

Always we pull away from what we see,
from what sees us. Dead children reach for us, we flee.

Rilke, without iPhone, but still prophet of our age.
Murderers are easy to understand, he wrote.
Who can endure these half-filled human masks?

Better Leatherface, whose mask masks nothing.
At least it is full. We only dream of existing.

How we squander our hours of pain, writing poems,
hiding from the world, in the darkness of the depthless page.

It takes more than one life to become who we are,
but we have just one dull life to sharpen bladed souls.

In my city of snow, of wind, of ice, of terror,
in my city of veins, of crows, of lakebed clay,
I walk without knowing where I am going,
walk forever beside who I think I am.
My children follow in my damaged footprints,
break snow and blur my once-perfect trail.

Once I wrote of wolves, of the holes
their notes would carve out of the sky.
Now I write of the throat that I offer
to whatever teeth willing to try.

Our cameras turn to the kill, turn to us,
and we livestream our own deaths,
timelines becoming traps.

Oh to be disconnected by a pure event.
Oh to be dead at last and know them endlessly,
all the stars.

Selfies

I wrote this poem that mentions Facebook, and after it gets published I will put it on Facebook and then one day my life will change.

Let's write a fucking poem!
You know what should be in it?
Desperation!

Maybe someone will read this poem!
Maybe someone important will read it,
like President Obama,
who I heard used to write poems
back in his college days, back when
he had nothing better to do
and his eyes still showed a spark of human life.

Maybe this poem will change my life.
I'll put it up on Facebook and you will like it,
and the president will like it, even though
he didn't really like it, it just seemed
like the political thing to do. Then one day,
months from now,
when my daughter does her Facebook chores,
she will like it and I will finally be happy.

I'm writing this poem on the bus,
while missing my daughter.

In the seat next to me, some guy is doing kung fu.
That's my life. Now it's in a poem!

Poems don't have time for ethics,
but maybe they *are* ethics. Or escapes from ethics.
Sit on that one for a while!
What are the ethics of a kung fu chop?
I hope he doesn't lean over to read this screen
so I don't have to find out.

If all the poets had to write
on buses, because they have three jobs and have to travel
from job to job so that they can afford bus fare to travel
between jobs, then we would have less poems.
I mean fewer poems, but also lesser poems.
Lesser poems, about how gardening's a metaphor for life.

In my garden, there are beets
I don't have time to pick and eat.
I don't have time, and my wife won't let me.
She says they will keep just fine. The frost, when it comes,
won't harm them. She's sick of eating beets
and sick of what they do to your piss, and anyways
(in Winnipeg, we say *anyways*, not *anyway*)
why can't we just pave the garden over
and rent it as a parking space?
The store beets are bigger and cheaper and less work.

These garden beets, which I don't get to eat,
 are just another job.

Actually, it's her garden and that's what I say.
It's not a metaphor.
It's real life, kids. We don't cotton to metaphors
around here, in this poem.

My daughter Jessie had a photo of James Franco on
her bedroom wall, so she tagged him in a selfie on
Instagram. When I saw this, I knew for certain and
forever that she was a funnier, smarter, and more com-
plex human being than I could ever hope to be. A while
later, James Franco used Instagram to try hooking up
with an underage girl like Jessie was then, which com-
plicates this poem. I thought about cutting it, but the
world complicates and destroys, and to pretend it does
not is a lie. Although I don't believe it has destroyed
this gift, and I don't believe that it can break our bond.

My daughter always texts James Franco right back.
They both belong in movies. Their brown eyes.
She tags him on Instagram, in school projects.
James Franco, what should I do? Tell me, please.

I act like you, James Franco, not in movies,
but act like I don't notice. I act well.
Like I don't notice eyes drift when she won't talk,
when there's something she won't tell me, when she hides.

James Franco, teach me to be perfect for her.
Teach me not to be annoying, to chill out.
Already I write poems, I teach my classes
how to write like James Franco and never sleep.

James Franco, put my daughter in a poem.
Put her in a poem like I do, write her letters
like I do. Write her letters. If she writes back,
tell me what she says, James Franco. She won't mind.

Many of these poems are about my daughter Jessie, so I asked her to help me edit this book. I asked her to put checkmarks or Xs on each page and said it was because I wanted her gut-response feedback as a reader, but actually I just wanted her to have a no-pressure way to tell me she was not comfortable with any poem about her going into the book. Her feedback was exceptional, and made me rethink and restructure the book and pull out many poems that I would have otherwise kept, and also she surprised me by not Xing any of the poems about her even though she is a private person. I felt that she was being very brave, so I am writing this in a title because I want her to know how much I appreciate her help but also how much I respect her for her strength.

When I wasn't with my daughter, I wrote poems.
Now – when I am with her – I watch her eyes drop
in the car, watch her lips move just a little, words wavering.

She doesn't trust her voice. She thinks I don't understand.
I do. Inside all things shimmers terror I can almost touch,
but will not touch. It belongs to her.

Poems for her come wrapped in shadows,
dark shapes fishlike under ice. If the ice melts,
and the poems leap free,

don't keep them. That's the worst thing
you could do. Pose for photos,
then release. I hope she never understands.

**This might be my last poetry book, since I might stop
writing poems. In many ways, this book explores what
poems mean to me and how I am not sure that they
mean what I want them to mean anymore. Please
understand. I am thirty-eight now, writing this title.
I was thirty-six when I wrote the first draft of this poem.
In those two years, the poem did not help. They were
two of the hardest years of my life, and the poem did
not help. It did not save me.**

I want to write poems for my children,
but I also want them to be happy.
I want them to not need poems.

I wrote this poem on an iPhone.
The future will not know
what that word means.

Beside dead rivers, we worship.
They flow into our open mouths,
swirl under our tongues,
douse out burning eyes.

Children, love this dear corpse of your father's.
Know the price that he has paid to live
and what it will cost him to leave life.
Tear the pages out of his last book.

The raven in this poem is an allusion to the raven in a poem that my daughter gave me on my birthday. The style of this poem owes a debt to her poem as well.

There's a wolf in my bedroom. It sings dark songs.
In the mornings, I find maggots. I'm afraid
of my dreams, of their reach. I'm afraid
of what these words mean. Come
and lie beside me, be a witness to this storm.

Explain these words to me. Come down,
Raven, come to my mouth, pick the flesh
from my dulled teeth. Be my witness.
Be eyes I have sewn shut against the winter.
Tell me all the frightful things I've done.

I have never been able to say what I mean or express how I feel. I became a writer because I thought that then I would know the perfect words and the perfect ways to tell you how I love you. My children. My beautiful ones. But I discovered that I am not that kind of writer. I am not the kind of writer who can say what he means. I am the kind of writer with a broken shard of glass inside of him. The glass moves throughout my body all the time. It cuts and cuts and nothing heals. It just keeps cutting and I write so that I do not have to pay so much attention to the pain.

I stalked castles for thousands of years.
I locked myself inside my head.
Still the angels refused to appear.

I will not take my own hand from fear.
I will not carry myself to bed.
Let me kiss you, my children, your dear

father invites you inside his terrible mind.
It is too late to be a human and in love.

I tell this same story in another book, where I break character and address the reader. But I tell it differently there, even though this is a true story. The story is true, and yet I have two different versions of it. But with my whole heart, my whole mind, my life, I swear to you that both are true. So what can we say about truth now? How can we live in this world?

When I was a child, psychotic,
I thought that I was Jesus.

I found a dead bird one day
and tried to bring it back to life.

I put my hands upon it.
Took it into my hands.

And it moved.
Flesh stirred, and I thought,

Here I am, here it is.
My miracle, at last.

Divinity, in this bird.
This child of God, of the blue, blue sky.

The bird twisted,
shedding its flesh,

and burst into a ball of squirming maggots.
I threw it down, back to the earth.

I have not believed in anything since.
I believe in nothing now.

**It has always been hard for me to plan for the future
because I always believed there was no future. It was
hard for me to have children because I want to believe
in a future for them. But I have never believed in the
future and it is hard to start believing now.**

Thom Yorke tells me the ice age is coming.
I believe his science. I trust my daughter,
mistrust my eyes. I believe in silence.

In death, we find true power.
All things want to hear their names,
hear what your red tongue has prepared

for the feast. Do not offer yourself
unless as meal. The woman at the front door
wants to save me, but she's wrong.

It takes something terrible to write a book, and I have wanted to write a book since I was young. It is the first thing that I remember wanting to do.

What is wrong inside the man who writes a book?
What sharp pencils have torn his once-blank pages?

I remember the days of my youth,
before the tall shadows rose and drew near.

Now the sound of grinding is low
and the light through the window has dimmed.

I sought to find words of delight
but only could write words of truth.

O my daughters, O my son, O love,
beware of anything beyond me.

The world's job is to weary flesh.
Of making many books there is no end.

*Help Me Because I Never
Learned To Hide*

I walk three hallways

In the first I carry
A cup of blood
And seek my name

In the second the moon
Cannot see
What it loves

In the third I hold hands
With a torch
And its shadow

I promised to meet you
But I'm gone

A writer writes to build a world he hates
Less than the world he knows

He flees the world
Flees into the page
But once there finds no freedom

Unlike the horrors of the world
The horrors of the page are all his fault

Standing inside the page
Standing outside the world
After all he sees beauty

But that beauty is lost to him now
He's stepped out of it, into the page

So I stand here now, inside this page
Frozen in a depthless field

Slashing my words across its bright snow
Burning myself for heat and to feel

I seek and find god in the snow
Bleeding like a cut dove in the snow

The paper cuts, the pain I need blooms inward
To sing this song I cut my throat with god

Midway through the journey of my life
I found myself inside a snow-bright field
I saw far in the distance my one life

I found myself inside a snow-bright field
And vowed I would return to what I loved
My daughters and my son and my dark lines

Hold those I love until they pull away
Help me, my mind betrays me all the time
I found myself inside a snow-bright field

To step out of the page, regain the world
Takes everything anyone ever gave
Takes every word a song could ever scream
Come with me on this long walk into cold

Come with me as the endless hallways twist
The hallways turn into snakes, swallow me
Come with me, all my children, follow me

Follow me into the den of teeth
Follow through the snake-mouths of my eyes
My hands are breaking, please hold my glass hands

Hold them together, hold my brittle fingers
Hold me tight until my poisoned sleep

I walk three hallways now, I know my name
I walk three hallways, each ends in a child
I walk until my song melts under me

Help me, teach me how to love this serpent
Help me, hold my face against its scales
Help me, there was never any world

Help me, my daughters, help me know myself
Help me, my son, help me sing this song
Help me write my way back to the world

This song has snared me, help me, help me please
A voice must carry it below the ice
I have to drown this song or I can't live

I have to touch the world with hands again
It looks so tempting held so far from me
I see it with the eyes grown from my palms

Help me be the father that won't die
Help me because I never learned to hide

If my daughter walked beside me
She would shiver in the cold

She would hold tight to herself
She would provide the perfect model

How a person should be

You should face the world and shiver
You should hold tight to yourself

You should walk close beside someone
Trust that someday it will warm

Notes

The National Gallery asks the question, 'Why create art?'

Thousands of years of written history have produced few good answers to this question. To make matters worse, I have tried to complicate those few good answers. Each sequence of poems adopts a differing approach, to complicate it in another way, considering the question both in terms of art's function in the public sphere and its engagement within private realms.

I do not have any answers, just this art.

§

The opening epigraph from Rilke's *Letters to a Young Poet* is from the translation by Stephen Mitchell, who also produced a beautiful translation of *The Book of Job* that was gifted to me for my daughter's first Christmas. However, my epigraph from *The Book of Job* is verse 19.2 from the King James Version.

Although many of these poems were written earlier, over the course of twenty years, this manuscript began to solidify when I started to write the poems in 'Group of Seven,' poems that take poetry itself, and how I relate to my poetry, and how the wider world relates to art, as their subject. These poems question the traditional purposes of poetry and address the various failures of art-making as a whole.

Each poem is titled after a member of the Group of Seven (including major affiliates, for a total of twelve poems). Since these artists have lost all sense of radicality due to their incorporation into the gallery system, these poems refuse to address their supposed subjects but instead mimic an aspect of their painterly approach by subverting conventional Canadian tropes in order to turn each poem against itself.

Many of the poems in this section, and in this book, owe a great debt to the influence of the poetry of Gary Barwin and Aaron Giovannone. The ending line of 'L. L. FitzGerald' ('This is my literal life') is from @mariah_reagan's Twitter feed, in response to a tweet by @mitchwelling ('I cry when I read my own poetry / I cry when I write my own poetry / I'm basically always crying').

'In the Room with the Light' was commissioned by Jennifer Gibson at the University of Winnipeg's Gallery 1C03 as a creative response to the work of Guy Maddin, specifically his collage works, *The Tender Fragments*, and his interactive website *Seances* (seances. nfb.ca). This long poem was originally published, in an earlier form, under the title 'Tender Fragments' in the Gallery 1C03 exhibition catalogue, *Moving Images*.

My poem extends Maddin's metaphor of art as a 'séance' that tries to enliven the past and exorcise its ghosts. Guy is a wonderfully sweet man who has always been kind to me. It was an honour to write this poem and I am thrilled to include it in a book that bears, on its back cover, kind words of support from Guy.

'Mixed Media' gathers poems that, with two exceptions, were drafted using their titles as Google search terms. Text was harvested from the online searches and collaged together to form loose drafts, which were then rewritten and expanded. Some of these poems are primarily composed of found text, while others are mainly constructed in a traditional method using found phrases as writing prompts.

One exception is 'I Am Something of a Salt,' which collects all of the phrases in Herman Melville's novel *Moby-Dick* that contain the word 'salt,' reproduced in order, without variations in the text (the title itself constitutes the first quotation).

'I can't be doing so badly, because I'm president, and you're not,' is a quotation from Donald J. Trump's interview with a *Time* reporter, published as 'Read President Trump's Interview With *Time* on Truth and Falsehoods' on March 23, 2017 (http://time.com/4710456/donald-trump-time-interview-truth-falsehood/).

In 'Food Court,' 'Joey's Only' begins with part of the final line from T. S. Eliot's 'The Love Song of J. Alfred Prufrock' to offer an imagined alternate ending. The music video for 'Call Me Maybe' is online at https://www.youtube.com/watch?v=fWNaR-rxAic and features a surprise ending in the manner of O. Henry. The poem 'KFC' takes its complete text from an actual advertisement on the website kijiji.ca and falls one sad syllable short of being a haiku.

'Leatherface Retrospective' contains ekphrastic poems relating primarily to the objects and artworks constructed by or surrounding the cannibal family in Tobe Hooper's film *The Texas Chain Saw Massacre*, which was released in 1974 and controversially acquired as part of the permanent collection of the Museum of Modern Art. Reportedly, Andrew Wyeth's 1948 painting *Christina's World*, also housed by MoMA, was one of Hooper's inspirations for the film.

'We cannot know his legendary face' rewrites the first line of Stephen Mitchell's translation of Rainer Maria Rilke's 'Archaic Torso of Apollo.' The poem 'Collage, Exegesis, Opening' contains some lines of dialogue from the Hooper film, in reaction to the sound collage that plays over the visual film-collage of the title credits. 'Blade Performance, Blood-Graffitied Van' also contains quotations from the film. The reference to Poe in that latter poem is to the short story 'The Purloined Letter' and its interpretation by psychoanalyst Jacques Lacan. The reference to Hill House in 'Nest of Spiders, Web that Captures Dreams' includes text distorted from the opening of Shirley Jackson's novel *The Haunting of Hill House*. The text of 'In the Red Room, Nothing Hides,' is taken from William Shakespeare's play *The Tempest*. Leatherface does not actually ring a dinner bell in the film, but I'm sure he does it from time to time.

The poems in 'Gift Shop' wear their inspirations or allusions openly, for the most part.

'iPhone Elegies' has its basis in *Duino Elegies* by Rainer Maria Rilke, as translated by Stephen Mitchell. The line 'I'm in an abusive relationship with poetry' is from Robin Richardson's Twitter feed (@robin_r_r). Many of the lines in this poem are unacknowledged transmutations or détournements of lines from Rilke, but the italicized lines have been reproduced verbatim.

The very long titles of the poems in 'Selfies' generally provide context for each poem. The song referenced in the line 'Thom Yorke tells me the ice age is coming' is 'Idioteque' by Radiohead, from the album *Kid A*. 'It takes something terrible to write a book' contains a number of quotations from *Ecclesiastes* 12 in the King James Version.

'Help Me Because I Never Learned To Hide' contains a series of references to Dante's *Inferno* and offers something of an answer to the question posed by the title of Sheila Heti's *How Should a Person Be?*

Acknowledgments

The National Gallery is dedicated to my children: Jessie, Claire, and Blake. My oldest daughter, Jessie, is the focus of many of its poems, and she also helped shape *The National Gallery*.

Jessie helped me think through and edit this manuscript, providing outstanding feedback at multiple stages. Initially, I admit, I just involved Jessie in the editing to give us something to do together where she didn't have to talk overmuch if not in the mood during her tumultuous teenage years. Almost immediately, she surprised me with outstanding and insightful feedback and editiorial suggestions and I shifted everything I was doing to move the manuscript more in line with the direction her reactions implied. This book truly would not have been possible without her help. She has more talent than I ever had and she was never afraid to let Dad know when his poems were just #fakedeep. Anything you love in this book owes its life to Jessie and anything you hate happened behind her back.

Jessie, I love you more than any poem could ever express. You are the strongest person I have ever known and I am so proud of my wonderful daughter. You will never understand how much you matter. My life meant nothing before you. Thank you for everything you are and for all the things I am because of you.

§

Thanks to many for their encouragement and support over the years, especially Derek Beaulieu, Christian Bök, Keith Cadieux, Natalee Caple, GMB Chomichuk, Kevin Connolly, Kevin

McPherson Eckhoff, Ryan Fitzpatrick, Dylan Fries, Catherine Hunter, Jeremy Leipert, Guy Maddin, Suzette Mayr, Maurice Mierau, Jay and Hazel MillAr, Kathryn Mockler, Saleema Nawaz, John Paizs, Adam Petrash, Michael Sanders, Patrick Short, Paul and Jacqueline Taylor, John Toone, and George Toles.

Special thanks to my patrons over at www.patreon.com/jonathanball, who help make my work possible: Candice Ball, Kevin McPherson Eckhoff (again), Reisha Hancox, Suzette Mayr (again), Thomas Ramsay, Darren Ridgley, Dan Twerdochlib, Bryce Warnes, and Mike Zastre.

Thanks to my family, especially my parents, grandparents, and brother Michael, for your tolerance of my strange pursuits, and to Mandy Heyens, for creating time and space for me to work.

Thank you to my editors Susan Holbrook and Alana Wilcox, and all the other wonderful people at Coach House Books (past, present, and future), who have helped to bring my books into the world.

The National Gallery owes its completion to the support of the Winnipeg Arts Council.

§

Many of these poems were previously published in earlier forms. I am immensely grateful to my various publishers and patrons: *AlbertaViews, BafterC, Best Canadian Poetry, The Capilano Review, CV2, Gallery 1C03, Grain, Matrix, The Maelstrom, NewPoetry.ca, Peter F. Yacht Club, Prairie Fire, Prism, Rogue Stimulus: The Stephen Harper Holiday Anthology for a Prorogued Parliament, The Rusty Toque, The Winnipeg Review, This Magazine, Touch the Donkey* and anyone else I forgot to include.

Jonathan Ball holds a PhD in English with a focus in Creative Writing and Canadian Literature. He is the author of seven books, including the previous poetry books *Ex Machina* (about how machines have changed what it means to be human), *Clockfire* (seventy-seven plays that would be impossible to produce), and *The Politics of Knives* (poems about cinema, narrative, and violence). He hosts the podcast Writing the Wrong Way, teaches writers to write better, edit faster, and stand out by doing things differently, and struggles to survive the Winnipeg winter.

www.JonathanBall.com
www.WritingTheWrongWay.com
www.TheNationalGallery.ca

Typeset in Oneleigh

Printed at the Coach House on bpNichol Lane in Toronto,
Ontario, on Zephyr Antique Laid paper, which was manufactured,
acid-free, in Saint-Jérôme, Quebec, from second-growth forests.
This book was printed with vegetable-based ink on a 1973 Hei-
delberg KORD offset litho press. Its pages were folded on a Baum-
folder, gathered by hand, bound on a Sulby Auto-Minabinda and
trimmed on a Polar single-knife cutter.

Edited by Susan Holbrook
Designed by Alana Wilcox
Cover image, 'Nature Morte' by Shana and Robert
    ParkeHarrison, courtesy of the artists

Coach House Books
80 bpNichol Lane
Toronto ON M5S 3J4
Canada

416 979 2217
800 367 6360

mail@chbooks.com
www.chbooks.com